AF679143

The Math of Financial Freedom

Weishan Xia

Copyright © 2025, 2026 by Weishan Xia

All Rights Reserved

This book is dedicated to:

Alec, Justin, Xinran, Xinyu, Sophie, Summer, Ann

Contents

Time is money.

— Benjamin Franklin

Preface

Many of us dream of achieving financial freedom—but the key question remains: How do we get there?

This book presents a simple and safe approach. While it may not be the fastest route, it requires no daily asset monitoring or active management. All you need is patience.

Most of the “rules,” “hypotheses,” and “theories” discussed in this book are not new; many have been around for quite some time. Although these ideas are not original to the author, the goal here is to weave them together into a coherent logical framework. This unified approach reveals a clear, secure, and accessible path to financial freedom—one that anyone can follow.

There are, of course, many ways to achieve financial independence: trading stocks, investing in real estate, building a business, and others. Occasionally, someone even wins the lottery. But those methods often require significant time, effort, and risk—or all three.

In contrast, this book offers what you might call a “lazy person’s financial plan”: a method that requires minimal time and effort, with almost no risk involved.

One important note: the strategies in this book are based primarily on U.S. laws and regulations and on historical data from the U.S. stock market. As such, they may not apply directly to other countries or regions. Even within the United States, investors should adapt these principles to suit their personal circumstances.

May each of us reach financial freedom as early as possible—so that both our minds and our bodies may enjoy greater happiness and freedom.

When I was young I thought that money was the most important thing in life; now that I am old I know that it is.

— Oscar Wilde

Chapter 1:

The 4 Percent Rule

Financial freedom is a state in which individuals no longer need to work for money to meet their living expenses. In straightforward terms, it implies that when you are not working, your financial concerns are alleviated because you have alternative sources of income. When work is not the only source of your income, you gain freedom, providing you with more time to participate in activities that you genuinely enjoy, such as traveling, writing, or meditating.

Determining the amount of money that you will need to achieve financial freedom hinges on understanding your monthly requirements—or more precisely, your annual needs, since some expenses are calculated annually. For instance, you might travel a few times a year, but not necessarily every month. Additionally, certain expenses, such as car insurance, may be paid annually or semi-annually, instead of monthly.

For example, suppose your total expenses for the past year amounted to $40,000. If you are 50 years old and hope to live to 80, that gives you 30 more years to account for in your financial planning. Does that imply that you will need $1.2 million to retire—$40,000 times 30? Not exactly, because following that formula, you would deplete all your savings on the last day of your life. Now the problem arises: if you run out of money when you are still alive, what should you do? Hope to live longer than 80? If so, should you hope to live to 85, 90, or 95? You have no control over that, so you will be left with a sense of uncertainty.

The good news is that, in reality, you may not need $1.2 million at all. In fact, you may be able to retire with much less. That is due to a principle known as the 4 Percent Rule, which asserts, *If you invest your savings in the U.S. stock market, and only withdraw up to 4 percent of the total each year, your money will never run out, no matter how long you live.* While it may sound too good to be true, it is indeed possible. Not only will your savings never deplete, but they will actually gradually grow. Nevertheless, it is crucial to note that the foundation of this rule is to invest your savings in the U.S. stock market, particularly in index funds, and not in individual stocks or traditional mutual funds. We will delve into this topic in more detail later; for now, just remember to focus on investing in index funds.

So, how does the 4 Percent Rule work? It is quite simple. Based on historical data, the average annual return of the U.S. stock market is 7 percent, while inflation is around 3 percent. Subtracting 3 percent from 7 percent gives you 4 percent. That implies that by withdrawing no more than 4 percent of your total investments each year, your money will not only last, but will grow at a rate of 3 percent, although the total value may not really change due to inflation.

Returning to the previous example: if

you require $40,000 per year, you will need to invest approximately $1 million in index funds. That approach will allow you to confidently withdraw up to 4 percent per year, or $40,000, which will ensure that your savings last indefinitely. In the end, you may even leave a substantial sum behind for your loved ones.

However, there are a few considerations to bear in mind when applying the 4 Percent Rule.

First, to emphasize the point once again, you will need to invest in index funds, not individual stocks or regular mutual funds.

Second, do not withdraw more than 4 percent of your total investments each year. Even if you plan not to take a single penny next year, you cannot withdraw 8 percent this year, since that will break the rule.

Third, if you encounter challenging years, such as when the stock market does not achieve a 7 percent return or even experiences a decline, consider reducing your expenses, since each dollar you withdraw at such times has a negative impact on the future value of your total investment.

If you prefer a more conservative approach, you can modify the 4 Percent Rule to a 3 Percent Rule, or even a 2 Percent Rule. However, be aware that this adjustment may require you to work a few more years to achieve your financial goals. The encouraging news is that once you have accumulated the savings required to fulfill the 4 Percent Rule, continuing to work becomes a relaxed and enjoyable experience, free from the fear of being laid off or getting upset about trivial matters at work. You will discover that your relationships with co-workers, your boss, or your clients become more harmonious, and your family relationships will undoubtedly improve as well. This is commonly referred to as the state of "semi-retirement."

Now that you understand the logic behind the 4 Percent Rule, you can use it to estimate how much money you need to retire, or to achieve financial freedom while continuing to work. Applying the 4 Percent Rule to the previous example once more: if you require $40,000 per year, you will need to save $1 million and invest all of it in index funds. That will enable you to confidently withdraw 4 percent each year, which will give you at least $40,000 for your annual expenses.

The question then becomes: how much should you save each year to accumulate that $1 million capital?

A straightforward approach would be to work backward. For example, if you aim to accumulate that amount in twenty years, you will need to save at least $50,000 per year ($1 million divided by 20). Even if you plan to achieve that in thirty years, you will still need to save at least $33,333 annually ($1 million divided by 30).

But what if you don't have that much extra money? For instance, if you can only save $10,000 each year, does that mean that you will need 100 years to save $1 million—which implies that you can never achieve financial freedom in your lifetime?

Fortunately, the answer is no. Even if

you can only save $10,000 per year, that doesn't mean you will need 100 years to accumulate $1 million. In fact, you won't even need 50 years. Thirty years will suffice. To explain why brings us to the next topic: compound interest!

Compound interest is the eighth wonder of the world. He who understands it, earns it ... he who doesn't ... pays it.

— Albert Einstein

Chapter 2:

The Rule of 72

Compound interest is a calculation method that not only applies interest to a principal amount, but also allows the accrued interest to generate additional interest. As interest compounds more frequently, wealth accelerates its growth, and over an extended period the profound impact of compounding becomes increasingly apparent.

Compound interest is a cornerstone in contemporary financial planning, yielding wealth growth known as the "compound effect"—which may significantly impact your financial wealth. For example, let us assume that you invest $10,000 at an annual return rate of 100 percent. If simple interest is applied, you will earn $10,000 annually, which will add up to $100,000 after ten years—"merely" ten times your initial investment.

However, with compound interest, in the initial year you will earn $10,000, doubling your wealth to $20,000. By the second year, that will double to $40,000, and that compounding effect will persist for ten years, resulting in your wealth growing to 2 to the power of 10—which is 1,024 times the initial principal! In other words, an initial $10,000 will burgeon to $10.24 million after a decade.

Due to that exponential growth, numerous ancient societies prohibited the practice of charging compound interest for loans. For instance, the Quran explicitly instructs Muslims not to “take usurious interest, multiplied and compounded” (Quran, 3:130). In 1571, England began permitting a maximum interest rate of 10 percent per year. Despite being set at only 10 percent, that rate still sparked ethical debates at the time. Consequently, the impacts of compound interest began to attract attention and consideration. In 1613, English mathematician Richard Witt published a groundbreaking book entitled *Arithmeticall Questions*, which presented a comprehensive analysis of the compound effect, marking a significant milestone in the history of compound interest.

Today, many countries have established restrictions on the interest rates that lenders can impose, often setting a ceiling around 30 percent. Interest rates surpassing that threshold are deemed usurious and are subject to prohibition in many jurisdictions. It is noteworthy that numerous credit card interest rates presently surpass 20 percent, and in some cases even reach 30 percent, which emphasizes the need for caution when you deal with such financial products.

Investors often seek higher annual returns, yet consistently achieving a 100 percent annual growth rate in economic activities is nearly impossible. In fact, a 10 percent annual return is often deemed quite favorable. As we have learned, with a 100 percent annual return, your capital doubles each year. But what if the annual return remains at only 10 percent? How long will it take for your capital to double? Besides employing the compound interest formula for accurate calculations, an expedient method known as the "Rule of 72" allows for rapid estimations.

The Rule of 72 works by dividing 72 by the annual return rate. For instance, with a 10 percent annual return rate, the calculation would be 72 divided by 10, or 7.2. That means your investment would take roughly 7.2 years to double. To be precise, if you use the compound interest formula, it will take you 7.273 years to double your investment. Likewise, with a 7 percent annual return rate, dividing 72 by 7 will take you about 10.286 years for your investment to double. Again, if you use the compound interest formula, it will take you 10.245 years to double your investment. Thus, the Rule of 72 yields fairly accurate approximations. Nevertheless, it is crucial to note that employing 72 as the divisor is suitable for general interest rates (e.g., 6 percent to 10 percent), but its accuracy notably diminishes for higher rates (e.g., 100 percent). "The Rule of 72 Table" in Appendix A, below, offers comprehensive information for reference.

In Chapter 1, "The 4 Percent Rule," you were left on a cliffhanger: if your savings were limited to $10,000 per year, would it require 100 years to amass $1 million? Absolutely not! By leveraging the compounding power highlighted in the present chapter, reaching $1 million will not require even 50 years, but only 30 years. For instance, if you invest $10,000 in U.S. index funds, since historical data indicate an average annual return rate of 7 percent in the U.S. stock market, your initial $10,000 will potentially grow to nearly $80,000 in 30 years. Indeed, using the Rule of 72 for a 7 percent return rate (72 divided by 7) indicates a little over 10 years for your initial capital to double. Put differently, your investment will double approximately three times over 30 years, approaching nearly eight times the original amount.

Furthermore, if you consistently invest $10,000 every year, you will accumulate the values of 30 separate investments made from the first to the thirtieth year. The sum of those investments will amount to slightly over $1,010,000. After subtracting the initial $300,000 ($10,000 times 30) that you invested, you will have accrued $710,000 in interest, or 2.37 times your capital. That clearly illustrates the remarkable power of the compound effect.

However, if you reduce the investment period, the results will reflect a different outcome in terms of accrued interest and overall growth of the investment. For instance, if you shorten the investment period from 30 years to 20 years, your final capital will amount to $438,650 by the end of the 20th year. After deducting the initial $200,000 ($10,000 times 20) that you invested, you will have accrued $238,650 in interest, nearly matching your initial capital. Similarly, if you shorten the investment period from 30 years to 10 years, your final capital will amount to $147,840 by the end of the 10th year. After deducting the initial $100,000 ($10,000 times 10) that you invested, you will have accrued $47,840 in interest, slightly less than half of your initial capital. Refer to the "Compound Interest Table" provided in Appendix B, below, for comprehensive details.

Indeed, the timeframe plays a pivotal role in illustrating the power of compound growth. The longer the investment period, the more pronounced the final outcome—even when the interest rate remains constant. In this context, the saying "time is money" is not just a motivational phrase; it is a mathematical reality. Starting early gives your investments more time to grow, and that makes all the difference.

You may still have some lingering questions. For example, why does the annual return rate of index funds closely match the historical average growth rate of the U.S. stock market, which is around 7 percent per year? Or what exactly distinguishes index funds from traditional mutual funds? And why should one choose index funds over individual stocks or actively managed funds?

All of these questions will be answered in the next chapter.

The Stock Market is designed to transfer money from the Active to the Patient.

— Warren Buffett

Chapter 3:

Index Funds

At the end of the previous chapter, several important questions remained unanswered. To answer those questions, we must first understand how stock market indices work, and then develop a clear grasp of what mutual funds truly are.

A stock price index, also known as a stock market index, represents the overall performance of a specific segment of the stock market. It is typically calculated as a weighted average of the stock prices of leading publicly traded companies listed on a country's major stock exchange, using a predefined algorithm. Well-known examples include the Dow Jones Industrial

Average and the Standard & Poor's 500 Index, both of which serve as benchmarks for the U.S. stock market's performance.

The Dow Jones Industrial Average is a stock market index calculated as the price-weighted average of 30 major companies listed on the New York Stock Exchange. Although it is one of the oldest and most widely followed indices, many experts argue that its limited scope—focusing on only 30 large corporations—fails to provide a comprehensive picture of the broader U.S. stock market. Additionally, because the Dow Jones Industrial Average uses a price-weighted method rather than a market-value-weighted one, it can misrepresent the relative importance of its component stocks, giving more influence to higher-priced shares, regardless of a company's actual size.

In contrast, the Standard & Poor's 500 takes a broader approach by including 500 widely held common stocks, which cover approximately 80 percent of the total U.S. stock market value. Compared to the Dow Jones Industrial Average, the Standard & Poor's 500 represents a much wider range of companies across various industries, which offers better diversification and a more accurate reflection of overall market trends. Moreover, it uses a market-value-weighted methodology, meaning each stock's influence on the index is proportional to the company's total market capitalization—providing a more realistic measure of each company's actual impact on the market.

Mutual funds serve as collective investment vehicles, which allows many individual investors to pool their money and have it managed by professional fund managers or institutions. The goal is to invest those combined funds strategically to generate returns for the investors. Because mutual funds typically manage large amounts of capital, they can diversify across numerous stocks and even multiple asset classes—thereby reducing risk and minimizing the impact of any single poor-performing investment. To support this strategy, mutual fund companies employ professional fund managers and research teams who conduct in-depth market analyses. This expertise enables a more informed understanding of the broader investment landscape and the specific factors affecting individual companies.

However, the active management strategy employed by mutual funds comes with both benefits and drawbacks. On the one hand, active managers aim to outperform the market by carefully selecting investments. On the other hand, frequent trading leads to higher transaction costs, and the salaries and commissions paid to fund managers and research teams can significantly increase overall expenses, which are ultimately borne by the investors. In response to these concerns, passive management—most notably through index funds—has emerged as a cost-effective alternative.

An index fund is a type of mutual fund that is designed to minimize tracking error by replicating the performance of a specific market index, such as the Standard & Poor's 500, Nasdaq 100, or others. To achieve this, index funds construct their portfolios by purchasing some or all of the stocks included in the target index, aiming to closely match its overall performance. As a result, many index funds deliver annual returns that closely align with the long-term average growth rate of the U.S. stock market—as noted, typically approximately 7 percent per year.

Compared to actively managed funds, index funds follow a passive investment strategy and therefore generally charge significantly lower fees. Actively managed funds often impose fees that range from 0.5 percent to 1.5 percent, and in some cases, even up to 2 percent. In contrast, index funds typically charge much lower fees—usually between 0.03 percent and 0.25 percent. Because index funds aim to passively track a specific index rather than outperform it, they involve minimal active trading. That not only reduces transaction costs, but also limits the influence of human judgment and error in day-to-day investment decisions.

You may be wondering whether greater human involvement in stock market investing—as seen in actively managed funds—is actually more effective, or if a more hands-off approach like that of index funds is the better strategy. After all, active fund managers are professionals, not amateurs. So the real question becomes: Can we trust them to consistently outperform the market? To explore this question, let's consider the following real-life example:

In February 2018, legendary investor Warren Buffett revealed that he had won a 10-year bet that he initiated in 2007. He had wagered $500,000 against professional money manager Ted Seides, asserting that, over the decade, a Standard & Poor's 500 index fund would outperform a portfolio of any five hedge funds handpicked by Seides. By the end of the bet in 2017, the returns on Seides's five hedge funds were 87.7 percent, 42.3 percent, 27.0 percent, 21.7 percent, and 2.8 percent. In comparison, the Standard & Poor's 500 index fund, Buffett's pick, gained a steady 125.8 percent. That outcome provided a powerful demonstration that even seasoned professionals can be easily outperformed by passive index funds.

In fact, data from the past two decades are even more striking. In the United States, fewer than 10 percent of all actively managed funds have consistently outperformed the market. What is even more perplexing is that the top 25 percent of active funds four years are no longer in that position today. That raises an important question: Did the successful funds outperform the market due to the skill of their managers, or was their success simply a matter of luck?

It's OK to have your eggs in one basket
as long as you control what happens
to that basket.

— Elon Musk

Chapter 4:

Survivorship Bias

Addressing the question at the end of the previous chapter, Burton Malkiel, a professor of economics at Princeton University, offered a compelling analysis in his 1973 book *A Random Walk Down Wall Street*.

Initially, Professor Malkiel introduced the "random walk hypothesis," which proposes that investment returns follow a random process. According to that hypothesis, stock market prices move in a manner similar to Brownian motion, which makes them inherently unpredictable. Professor Malkiel then examined several popular investment strategies—such as technical analysis and fundamental analysis—pointing out their clear limitations. Both approaches, he noted, attempt to predict a future that is essentially random by relying on past data or current market conditions. Ultimately, Professor Malkiel concluded that, for most investors, those strategies tend to produce returns that are worse than the ones achieved through passive investment approaches.

Certainly, some dissenting voices have challenged Professor Malkiel's views, often pointing to enduring investment legends like Warren Buffett and Peter Lynch. A reasonable explanation for the success of these investors is that they often have access to superior information, which enables them to outperform the market. For example, Lynch noted that he frequently met with CEOs and other senior managers from companies that were seeking investments from his firm, Fidelity Investments. Those interactions, he said, gave him exclusive insights that were not readily available to the general public.

Nevertheless, despite having access to superior information, most professional investors—including hedge fund manager Ted Seides, who made the bet against Buffett—still struggle to consistently outperform the market. From a probabilistic perspective, the continued success of a very small number of investors largely comes down to chance. Over time, there will always be individuals who outperform the market, but they are statistical outliers in the investment world.

Unfortunately, due to selection bias, the public tends to focus only on rare successes, often overlooking the much larger group of investors who do not succeed. This phenomenon is known as "survivorship bias."

Survivorship bias is a logical fallacy that occurs when excessive attention is paid to "survivors," while "losers" are overlooked, which leads to faulty conclusions. A classic example of avoiding survivorship bias came from Abraham Wald, a statistics professor at Columbia University during World War II. Wald applied the concept of survivorship bias to develop strategies for minimizing damage to bombers based on the patterns of bullet holes found on aircraft returning from missions.

After examining the damage on the returning planes, Professor Wald recommended reinforcing the areas that showed the least damage, rather than those with the most bullet holes. His reasoning was that the bullet holes marked sections where planes could sustain hits and still return safely. In contrast, the areas with little or no damage were likely critical spots. If those were hit, he reasoned, the planes would not make it back, and thus were not represented in the data. Based on that insight, Professor Wald advised strengthening those vulnerable areas that, if struck, could cause fatal damage. His work had a profound impact on the emerging field of operations research during that time.

From Malkiel's "random walk

hypothesis" to Wald's concept of "survivorship bias," it becomes clear that even if a monkey were to randomly pick stocks, its performance would likely be no better—and no worse—than that of an individual or institution that selected stocks "carefully." Does this mean that investing requires no skill or strategy? Certainly not. For example, in *A Random Walk Down Wall Street*, Professor Malkiel offered two practical strategies to help reduce investment risk: diversification and dollar-cost averaging.

Diversification is a simple concept: Don't put all your eggs in one basket. But how many baskets should you use? The key is to find a balance—not too few, and not too many. According to Professor Malkiel's research, diversifying across approximately 50 baskets can reduce risk by more than 60 percent. Beyond that, increasing the number to 500 baskets does not significantly lower risk further. In other words, diversifying into approximately 50 different investments is sufficient.

When it comes to choosing baskets, the approach is straightforward: opt for a random selection! If making individual decisions feels overwhelming or managing 50 separate investments seems daunting, there is a convenient solution: an index fund. And if investing in only one index fund feels too simplistic, you can diversify further by investing in several index funds from different countries and markets, allocating your investments across them to reduce risk even more.

Dollar-cost averaging is an investment

strategy whereby a fixed amount of money is invested regularly in a particular asset at set intervals. The goal of dollar-cost averaging is to reduce the impact of market volatility on an investor's overall returns. For example, investing $10,000 annually in an index fund over 30 years is a practical illustration of this approach.

To further reduce risk, consider breaking that $10,000 into smaller portions that you invest gradually over time. For example, you could divide the $10,000 into 12 equal parts, investing $833.33 each month. This approach means that if the fund's value drops after a purchase, your losses are limited, since you haven't committed your entire capital all at once. Additionally, investing incrementally allows you to buy more shares when prices are lower, which helps to reduce your average cost over time.

Another benefit of dollar-cost averaging is that it eliminates the stress of trying to time the market or deciding the best day to invest. This method promotes simplicity by encouraging regular disciplined investing—often through automated contributions.

In summary, combining index fund investing with dollar-cost averaging makes the investment process safer, more manageable, and less stressful.

Do not save what is left after spending,
but spend what is left after saving.

— Warren Buffett

Chapter 5:
The 30 Percent Rule

In Chapter 1, "The 4 Percent Rule," we calculated the amount of savings needed for retirement by estimating annual living expenses. For instance, if your projected retirement expenses will be $40,000 per year, you would need to accumulate $1 million before retiring—investing that money primarily in index funds. After retirement, by withdrawing roughly 4 percent annually (about $40,000), your portfolio can potentially last indefinitely, offering long-term financial freedom for the rest of your life.

In Chapter 2, "The Rule of 72," we explored how to leverage compound interest to reach the $1 million retirement goal. The chapter illustrated that by consistently investing $10,000 per year in index funds, you could accumulate $1 million in just 30 years.

It is worth noting that, in the previous example, the annual $10,000 investment in index funds represents exactly 1 percent of the $1 million retirement goal. That aligns with the 4 percent annual withdrawal rate in retirement, creating a 1:4 ratio between pre-retirement saving and post-retirement spending. In other words, if you maintain this 1:4 ratio—saving 20 percent of your income and spending the remaining 80 percent every year—your lifestyle after retirement can remain largely unchanged. This concept is commonly known as the 20 Percent Rule for savings.

However, the 20 Percent Rule has a critical shortcoming: it does not account for inflation before retirement. Assuming an average annual inflation rate of 3 percent, the cost of living 30 years from now will be approximately 2.43 times higher than it is today—calculated as 1.03 raised to the power of 30. In other words, to preserve your future purchasing power, you would actually need to save and invest around 48.6 percent of your income—nearly half—rather than just 20 percent. That adjustment reflects the need to match the anticipated 2.43-fold increase in expenses over three decades.

If the idea of saving nearly half your income feels overwhelming, don't worry. There are two favorable factors thar we haven't accounted for yet.

The first favorable factor is the general trend of income growth over time, which—ideally—outpaces inflation. The second favorable factor is that increasing your savings rate (beyond 20 percent) naturally reduces your spending rate (below 80 percent), which in turn lowers the total amount you will need in retirement. Since inflation affects expenses annually, the required retirement savings adjust each year as well. We will refer to this evolving amount as your "target savings."

Let's assume that your annual income grows at 4 percent, slightly outpacing the 3 percent inflation rate. After careful calculations, it becomes clear that the required savings rate should increase from 20 percent to 28.1 percent. That adjustment will allow you to accumulate approximately $2.189 million, slightly exceeding the target savings of $2.181 million by year 30. For a detailed breakdown, refer to the "28.1 Percent Savings Table" in Appendix C, below.

In simple terms, by consistently saving and investing around 30 percent of your income, it is entirely possible to achieve financial freedom within 30 years—even in the face of steady inflation. Saving and investing around 30 percent of your income will give rise to a more reliable guideline: the 30 Percent Rule for savings.

It is important to recognize that when you withdraw funds from your investment account after retiring, you may be subject to a capital gains tax. Fortunately, in addition to using standard brokerage accounts to purchase index funds, you can also invest through retirement accounts, which offer tax advantages that can help you to avoid capital gains taxes.

In the United States, the federal government outlines retirement benefit regulations in Section 401(k) of the Internal Revenue Code—commonly referred to as a 401(k) plan. One key benefit of a 401(k) is that you add to it with pre-tax income, meaning that your contribution to the plan is deducted from your paycheck before taxes are applied. Moreover, taxes on both 401(k) contributions and investment gains are deferred until you make withdrawals—typically after the age of 59½, at which point they are taxed as ordinary income.

Moreover, when employees contribute a portion of their salary to a retirement account, many large companies offer employer matching, typically up to a certain limit. For example, with a 50 percent match, the company contributes $0.50 for every $1 the employee invests, which results in a total of $1.50 going into the employee's retirement account. However, retirement accounts come with age-related withdrawal restrictions, so accessing funds before the designated age of 59½ incurs penalties and additional taxes.

In the United States, Health Savings Accounts provide valuable opportunities for investment and financial management. These accounts offer significant tax advantages; namely, contributions are made with pre-tax dollars and are exempt from both capital gains taxes and income taxes. However, it is important to remember that the funds in Health Savings Accounts must be used for qualified medical expenses. If you withdraw money for non-medical purposes before age 65, you will owe income tax plus a 20 percent penalty. After you turn 65, the penalty no longer applies, and withdrawals for non-medical expenses are taxed as ordinary income.

In reality, there are many paths to financial freedom, including stock trading, real estate investment, entrepreneurship, and more. Occasionally, some individuals even achieve financial freedom by winning the lottery. However, it is important to remember the concept of survivorship bias—focusing only on the success stories, while ignoring the much larger group who do not succeed, can create a distorted view. Aside from the rare chance of hitting the jackpot, what are the realistic odds of success when you start a business?

According to data from the U.S. Bureau of Labor Statistics, about 20 percent of new businesses fail within two years, roughly 45 percent within five years, nearly 65 percent within ten years, and approximately 85 percent within fifteen years. It is understandable that many entrepreneurs view themselves as part of the fortunate 15 percent who survive after fifteen years. However, even within that select group, a critical question remains: Can the return on investment from your business consistently outperform the typical 7 percent annual return of index funds? Moreover, even if your business does achieve higher returns, you miss the convenience and simplicity of investing in index funds with just a few taps on a smartphone or computer. Instead, you have to invest significant time and effort in running your business.

When it comes to real estate investment and rental property management, aside from regular tenant turnovers, you may receive calls at any hour requesting repairs—whether for clogged drains, leaky roofs, or other maintenance issues. If you genuinely enjoy these hands-on responsibilities, that is a different story. However, for individuals who prioritize maximum autonomy on their path to financial independence, consistently investing in index funds offers an optimal "hands-off" or "lazy person's" retirement strategy.

Less is more.

— Mies Van Der Rohe

Chapter 6:

The Minimalist Rule

In the preceding chapter, we discussed the 30 percent savings guideline as a strategy to counteract inflation. It is important to clarify that this rule does not suggest saving exactly 30 percent of your income, while spending the remaining 70 percent. Rather, the 30 percent guideline represents a baseline—just enough to maintain your desired lifestyle after you retire. To achieve early retirement or build greater financial resilience for weathering economic downturns, it is essential to save more than this baseline and start your savings journey as early as possible.

So, how much can increasing your

savings rate accelerate your path to retirement? In the previous example—assuming a 3 percent annual inflation rate and 4 percent income growth—maintaining a 30 percent savings rate could achieve financial freedom within 30 years. But what if you increase your savings rate by 10 percentage points, raising it to 40 percent? How would that impact the timeline for reaching financial independence?

Building on our earlier discussion of inflation's impact, it is important to consider two favorable factors. First, incomes generally rise over time—ideally outpacing inflation. Second, increasing your savings rate (for example, from 30 percent to 40 percent) naturally lowers your consumption rate (from 70 percent to

60 percent), which reduces the total amount you will need to accumulate for retirement. Keep in mind that the required annual savings amount varies over time and is referred to as "target savings."

By factoring in both the positive and negative elements and performing meticulous recalculations, we produce an updated table that shows annual cumulative savings ("balance") alongside corresponding "target savings." Those data are available in Appendix D, below, entitled "40 Percent Savings Table." The appendix clearly shows that with a 40 percent savings rate, your cumulative savings in year 22 ($1.469 million) exceed the target savings for that year ($1.437 million). In other words, increasing your savings rate from 30 percent to 40 percent enables you to achieve financial freedom 8 years earlier.

Furthermore, by increasing your savings rate to 50 percent, you can achieve financial freedom by year 17. That represents a further reduction of 5 years, compared to the 22 years required at a 40 percent savings rate. Detailed information about this can be found in Appendix E, below, entitled "50 Percent Savings Table." Remarkably, by boosting your savings rate to 70 percent, you can attain financial freedom as early as year 9, even with a total accumulation of roughly $518,240 during that period. For a full breakdown of this, see Appendix F, below, entitled "70 Percent Savings Table."

It is natural to question the feasibility of these calculations. Even if the numbers are accurate, maintaining such high savings rates can be challenging for many people. However, by embracing minimalism and simplifying your lifestyle, achieving financial freedom in a shorter time frame becomes a realistic—and attainable—goal, rather than an impossible mission.

Originating as an art movement in the 1960s, minimalism has since evolved into a lifestyle, a consumption philosophy, and a value system centered on intentional decluttering decision-making. At its core, minimalism embraces the idea that "less is more," encouraging the removal of unnecessary, interchangeable, and unappreciated possessions ("less") to foster a richer life experience ("more"). That approach enhances visual appeal, creates more living space, and reduces needless consumption.

Minimalism encompasses a broad spectrum of ideas, giving rise to many guiding principles. However, when it comes to achieving financial freedom, one simple rule often suffices: curb impulsive consumption. By cutting back on excess spending, you not only increase your savings and investment potential—harnessing the power of compounding—but also reduce your "target savings" because a minimalist lifestyle lowers your required retirement expenses. It is like moving toward a goal while the goal itself draws nearer. Interestingly, the faster you advance, the quicker the goal seems to come within reach.

In an extreme scenario, if you embraced

an even more minimalist lifestyle than the average minimalist—effectively having zero expenses—you would achieve financial freedom immediately, without ever needing to work a day. Of course, achieving zero expenses in reality is impossible, but legendary figures like superheroes might effortlessly accompany such a feat. For example, superheroes often have the ability to instantly travel anywhere, saving massive costs on transportation, including car payments and insurance. They typically live in modest apartments, avoiding mortgages and property insurance. Despite their iconic looks, many superheroes maintain a consistent wardrobe, eliminating frequent clothing purchases. Additionally, many superheroes prefer solitude or embrace singlehood; even those with companions usually choose a childless lifestyle.

It is no surprise that most superheroes do not hold conventional jobs, given their minimal expenses and lifestyle. In fact, when they do have a job, it often serves as a cover to protect their true identities. The key point is that they are not dependent on work and naturally live in a state of financial freedom. Viewing their global travel and their altruism as active charitable engagement sheds light on their actions and motivations. These aspirations perfectly mirror what many of us hope to achieve after attaining financial freedom. Seeing this, wouldn't you want a life like theirs? If so, what is stopping you? Start by saving more, spending less, and investing earlier!

Spending less does not mean depriving yourself of basic needs. It is about mastering your desires to achieve maximum happiness while using minimal financial resources. For example, instead of buying a brand-new recreational vehicle that sits idle in your driveway, exposed to the elements and used only a few times a year, you could rent one for a cross-country trip. Similarly, you might charter a yacht for deep-sea fishing excursions, rather than purchasing an extravagant yacht solely for vanity—mooring it at a distant harbor and hiring staff to maintain it. It is important to remember that such assets rapidly depreciate over time. Cars and yachts fall into that category of consumer goods rather than investments, due to their inherent tendency to lose significant value.

Hedge fund manager Bill Perkins introduced the concept of "Die with Zero" in his book of the same name. His idea is that when we pass away, we should have no remaining wealth, since we used our resources fully to live a rich and fulfilling life. While that notion may seem to contradict minimalism, it actually aligns with its core principles. At its essence, minimalism seeks to eliminate waste—not just financial, but also the waste of time and life potential. Perkins argues that spending the bulk of our time earning money without enjoying its rewards before death is, in itself, a waste—of both time and money. Money is merely a tool; the true objective is to enjoy life. Yet, in the pursuit of wealth, many individuals inadvertently sacrifice the very experiences and fulfillment they are striving for.

Of course, it is neither necessary nor realistic to spend every last cent at the moment of your death. Fortunately, this book presents a balanced and sustainable approach—one that allows you to achieve financial freedom, while still leaving behind meaningful resources for your loved ones.

To conclude, consider this anonymous quote:

“Stop being fooled by the illusion of wealth. Big houses, expensive cars, designer brands, and a flashy lifestyle are not wealth—they are debt. True wealth is time, freedom, options, and health.”

Great investing requires a lot of delayed gratification.

— Charlie Munger

Chapter 7:

Delayed Gratification

In the preceding chapter, I emphasized that reducing impulsive consumption is a foundational principle of minimalism. Failing to follow that rule can significantly delay your journey toward financial freedom. Nevertheless, many people struggle to apply that rule in practice—often falling into impulsive buying habits and shopping sprees. That brings us to an important question: Is self-control something we are born with, or is it a skill we develop over time? And if it is developed, can it be strengthened through training? To explore these questions, let's begin with the famous "marshmallow experiment."

The Stanford marshmallow experiment, conducted in 1972 by psychologist Walter Mischel, explored the concept of delayed gratification. In the study, children were given a simple choice: they could have one small reward immediately—typically a marshmallow—or wait for a short period (15 minutes) to receive two rewards instead. During the waiting period, the researcher left the children alone in a room, one by one, with a single marshmallow in front of them. If the children resisted the temptation to eat the marshmallow, they would receive an additional treat—either a second marshmallow or a pretzel stick, depending on their preference. Mischel conducted the experiment with over 600 children from a Stanford-affiliated kindergarten. The results were revealing: only approximately 30 percent of the children were able to wait the full 15 minutes to earn the larger reward.

Follow-up studies revealed that the children who were able to delay gratification tended to experience better life outcomes over time, including higher SAT scores, greater educational attainment, healthier body mass index, and other positive achievements. In other words, those children who resisted the immediate reward demonstrated stronger self-discipline or self-control, and were more likely to be viewed as "successful" later in life. Of course, it is important to acknowledge that the definition of success is inherently subjective and cannot be reduced to academic performance or conventional lifestyle choices. However, that broader philosophical question lies beyond the scope of this book and will not be explored further here.

A key question then becomes: What determines our capacity for self-control? First, Professor Mischel found that self-control is closely linked to age. For instance, children under the age of 4 rarely manage to wait for the second reward, whereas by age 12, approximately 60 percent are able to delay gratification. Gender also plays a role. Among children of the same age and facing the same level of temptation, girls generally demonstrate greater self-control than boys. However, both age and gender are factors beyond our immediate control. So, the more important question is: Are there factors that can be improved through our own efforts?

Yes, there are such factors, one of which is self-confidence—a trait that Professor Mischel found to be positively correlated with self-control. Self-confidence refers to your belief in your ability to succeed through personal effort. There are many ways to build self-confidence, but one key method is through rational analysis—specifically, calculating the probability of success. The higher the calculated likelihood of success, the more confident you become in your ability to achieve it.

In previous chapters, I used logic and mathematical reasoning to show that financial freedom is far from a distant dream. If you have grasped the underlying principles and verified the numbers in the appendices by using the provided formulas, then that understanding can play a powerful role in reinforcing your confidence. With confidence comes clarity—and with clarity, self-discipline or self-control become easier to cultivate.

Professor Mischel also discovered that self-control is correlated with stress. In other words, the higher the stress level, the weaker the self-control; and the lower the stress level, the stronger the self-control. That helps to explain why people often engage in impulsive or irrational behaviors, such as overeating, excessive drinking, or compulsive shopping, when they experience emotional distress, such as after a romantic breakup. While external stressors are often beyond your control, what is within your power is how you manage and respond to stress when it arises. Two of the most widely recognized strategies for stress reduction are physical exercise and meditation. Although many people have experienced the benefits of exercise in managing stress, far fewer have explored the use of meditation to calm the mind and curb impulsivity. Later in this chapter, I will focus on that topic, offering a deep dive into how meditation can strengthen self-control and support long-term well-being.

From a neuroscience perspective, Professor Mischel outlined a foundational strategy for strengthening self-control: inhibiting the brain's "hot system" and activating its "cool system." The hot system is rooted in your brain's limbic structures, such as the hippocampus and the amygdala, both of which govern instinctual impulses and survival-driven emotions. The hot system generates fast, automatic responses, which often demand immediate gratification without regard for long-term consequences. In contrast, the cool system resides in your prefrontal cortex, the brain's center for higher-order thinking, which is slower to respond, but capable of deliberate reflection, reasoning, and planning. When it is activated, the cool system shifts your mindset from reactive and emotional to calm and rational, allowing you to override impulsive urges and make more thoughtful decisions. In essence, self-control is your ability to suppress the quick, emotionally charged reactions of your hot system by engaging the cooler, more reflective part of your brain—enabling delayed gratification and progress toward long-term goals.

In fact, what Professor Mischel described as the "hot system" is not a new concept. As early as the nineteenth century, the German philosopher Arthur Schopenhauer proposed that all human actions are ultimately governed by the "will to live"—the fundamental force that drives all desires. According to Schopenhauer, while we may appear to have conscious control over our words and actions, in reality our behaviors are steered by that underlying will, expressed through various desires.

If the concept of "will" still feels abstract to you, Richard Dawkins's book The Selfish Gene offers additional clarity. Interpreting Schopenhauer's "will to live" through the lens of evolutionary biology, Dawkins argues, helps to demystify it: our actions are shaped by biological imperatives that are aimed at survival and reproduction. Put simply, Schopenhauer's "will" aligns closely with what Professor Mischel later termed the "hot system"—a biologically rooted, emotionally charged force that propels us toward immediate gratification.

Schopenhauer further argued that all of nature—including humankind—is the manifestation of an insatiable will, and that it is through this will that humans experience suffering. It is our constant craving for more that lies at the root of this suffering. If we accept that the essence of human nature is the "will to live," and that suffering arises from this will—deeply embedded in our genes—then attempting to resist it directly may seem futile. However, Schopenhauer offered a subtle yet profound insight: the will does not control our actions directly, but rather indirectly through desire. That distinction is crucial, for it suggests that to free ourselves from the suffering caused by the will, we must eliminate desire itself—severing the link between the will and our actions. Only by dissolving that intermediary can one hope to transcend the grip of the will and attain genuine inner liberation. Thus, Schopenhauer's proposed solution to combat the will was asceticism, although he did not prescribe any specific method for achieving it.

So, are there ways to eliminate human desire? Indeed, there are—and one of the most effective is meditation. In *The Science of Meditation*, the present writer explains that the essence of meditation lies in maintaining conscious awareness, while allowing the body to enter a sleeplike state. During that process, the sensory nerves gradually shut down as the body enters sleep. If, like ancient Asian philosophers, such as Buddha, we believe that all desires come from the senses, when hearing, seeing, smelling, tasting, and touching are shut down, all desires will disappear with them. While this simplistic and straightforward view may differ from modern biology's explanations of desire, meditation undeniably reduces desire, thereby bringing inner peace, clarity of thought, and spiritual fulfillment to the meditator.

It is evident that Schopenhauer's proposal of asceticism is a purely rational solution to human suffering, relying entirely on reason and self-control to combat desires. Meditation, on the other hand, ingeniously sidesteps this direct confrontation with desires. By inducing the body into a sleeplike state and gradually shutting down sensory nerves, meditation naturally dissolves desires from within. As Sun Tzu said in The Art of War, "The greatest victory is that which requires no battle."

In fact, during meditation—or even normal sleep—not only do the sensory nerves gradually shut down, but the motor nerves do as well. Additionally, the brain suppresses the sympathetic nervous system while activating the parasympathetic nervous system, guiding the body into a deeply relaxed, sleeplike state. The sympathetic nerves are responsible for fight-or-flight. When these nerves are stimulated, that is manifested by, among other things, a rapid heartbeat, faster breathing, dilated blood vessels, sweating, and dilated pupils—signs that the "hot system" is engaged. Conversely, the parasympathetic nerves are responsible for recuperation and digestion. When the parasympathetic nerves are stimulated, that slows down the heartbeat, decreases myocardial contractility, shrinks the pupils, contracts smooth muscles, strengthens gastrointestinal peristalsis, relaxes the skeletal muscles, and increases saliva and tear secretion—effectively deactivating the "hot system."

At this point, you might wonder: if the explanation above shows how meditation and sleep suppress the hot system, how exactly is the cool system activated? In fact, the hot and cool systems function like two ends of a seesaw: when one is pushed down, the other naturally rises. However, during normal sleep, we lose consciousness, so the cool system cannot be activated. Meditation differs from normal sleep in that it induces a sleeplike state while maintaining consciousness. That subtle yet crucial difference allows meditation to suppress the hot system while simultaneously activating the cool system. As a result, in a meditative state, we can make more rational and sound decisions when faced with challenges or temptations.

Of course, the benefits of meditation extend far beyond that. For a deeper exploration of the psychological and physiological advantages, please refer to *The Science of Meditation*, since I will not delve into those details here.

In conclusion, in the present book I have laid out a clear, practical, and reliable path to financial freedom. Besides that, I have provided concrete strategies for strengthening self-control—which is crucial for staying focused and not getting distracted on your financial journey. By applying the "mathematical rules" introduced here, you can precisely calculate your timeline to financial independence, gaining both clarity and confidence.

If you have read this far, what are you

waiting for? Take action now: start saving, investing, and meditating! May each of you soon attain financial freedom, bringing greater happiness to both your mind and your body.

The main vice of capitalism is
the uneven distribution of prosperity.
The main vice of socialism is
the even distribution of misery.

— Winston Churchill

Chapter 8:

The Capitalism Rule

In the earlier chapters, I focused on ways to achieve personal financial freedom from an individual perspective. In this chapter, I will adopt a broader view to examine the root causes of wealth disparities among different groups, regions, and even nations. That shift of perspective is not meant to complicate the book, but to offer insight into why the strategies outlined in this book effectively build wealth. Furthermore, we will explore whether alternative paths to financial freedom might exist that are more advantageous or better suited to certain individuals.

Throughout most of human history, people lived largely self-sufficient lives marked by low productivity and slow wealth accumulation. However, the Industrial Revolution drastically altered that trajectory. That transformative era significantly boosted productivity, which evolved through stages of mechanization, electrification, and informatization, which are now ushering in an age of intelligence. Thanks to these advancements, humanity has accumulated more wealth in the past few centuries than in all the previous eras combined. Yet, alongside that tremendous growth of wealth, disparities have also widened—both between socioeconomic groups within societies and between wealthy and less wealthy nations.

It is important to recognize that the

widening wealth gaps do not necessarily imply that poor individuals and nations are becoming poorer. Rather, both the poor and the rich may be accumulating wealth, but the rich are doing so at a significantly faster pace. But what drives that phenomenon? While it is commonly said that "labor creates wealth," many individuals amass wealth without directly engaging in physical labor. They are called "capitalists." Beyond capitalists, there are also individuals who acquire wealth through power and force, or by inheritance, but they lie outside the scope of this discussion. Here, I will focus on the capitalist class, carefully exploring how its members accumulate wealth without physical labor, as I uncover the fundamental difference between their method and the principle that "labor creates wealth."

The term capitalists refers to individuals who possess capital. At its core, capital is money that has the ability to generate more money. While money can be simply viewed as cash, capital distinguishes itself by representing funds that are capable of producing returns. In other words, capital involves a combination of funds and business insight. Specifically, beyond just having money, capitalists must apply their intellect—or leverage the intellect of others—to develop ideas that utilize existing funds to create new value. That process lies at the heart of capital creation. When capitalists rely on the ideas of others, they typically pay for those ideas in advance or offer the others a share of equity—often in the form of stock.

Typically, business profits are distributed based on the amount of capital invested, meaning that those individuals who contribute more capital naturally receive a larger share of the returns. However, the vast majority of people neither invest significant capital nor receive any form of equity. As a result, their primary or even sole source of income is labor. That lack of access to capital income lies at the heart of the fundamental imbalance between capital and labor, and it is this imbalance that drives the widening wealth gap in modern society.

From a historical perspective, even when wages keep pace with inflation, they consistently fall behind the overall rate of economic growth—and lag even further behind the typical returns on capital. Modern economic data show that the average annual rate of return on capital investments ranges between 4 and 5 percent, while the long-term average gross domestic product (GDP) growth rate is only about 1 to 2 percent per year. This means that the majority of benefits of economic growth accrue to capital owners. French economist Thomas Piketty clearly articulated that dynamic in his book *Capital in the Twenty-First Century*, arguing that when the rate of return on capital (r) exceeds the rate of economic growth (g), wealth inevitably accumulates with capital.

It is important to note that the figures mentioned above have already been adjusted for inflation. As previously discussed, the average annual return of the U.S. stock market is approximately 7 percent, while the average annual inflation rate hovers around 3 percent. Subtracting inflation from market returns yields a real return of approximately 4 percent—which is consistent with the global average rate of return on capital investment (between 4 and 5 percent).

Furthermore, the Rule of 72—a simple way to estimate the doubling time of an investment— vividly illustrates the disparity: capital that grows at an annual rate of 4 percent will double in just 18 years (72 ÷ 4), while an average worker's wealth, which grows at 1 percent annually, would take a staggering 72 years to double (72 ÷ 1). That stark contrast underscores a crucial reality: although both capital owners and wage earners may benefit from economic growth, the gap between them will inevitably continue to widen over the years.

For a long time, scholars and researchers have sought to understand why economic income in human society tends to disproportionately favor capital. A common explanation attributes that imbalance to the greed of capitalists, who seek to appropriate the surplus value created by labor. However, in a free-market system, both labor and capital play essential roles in creating income, and their respective rewards—wages and profits—are largely determined by market forces, rather than being dictated solely by capitalists. That raises a critical question: In a fully competitive and unrestricted market, why do capitalists still manage to capture the lion's share of the income generated through the joint efforts of labor and capital?

One significant reason is the relative scarcity of capital compared to labor in the marketplace. In general, the scarcer a factor of production is, the higher its market price. Because capital is relatively scarce, it commands greater bargaining power than labor. In contrast, standard labor—which is abundant—typically has weaker bargaining power. That said, certain specialized forms of labor may possess a degree of irreplaceability, granting them relatively greater bargaining power, as is often the case with members of the middle class.

Another significant factor is the substantially higher risk associated with capital investment compared to the relative stability of a conventional 9:00-to-5:00 job. As previously noted, data from the U.S. Bureau of Labor Statistics show that approximately 20 percent of new businesses fail within two years, and around 45 percent within five years. Given those risks, it is reasonable to expect that if the return on capital investment falls below a certain threshold, it will significantly dampen the willingness of capitalists and entrepreneurs to launch new ventures. At the same time, that will also discourage reinvestment into existing businesses, thereby limiting their capacity to grow and expand. Ultimately, that could lead to a slowdown in overall economic growth.

In summary, a fundamental outcome of free-market capitalism is the gradual concentration of wealth in the hands of capital owners, which leads to an ever-widening gap between the rich and the poor. While the rates of economic growth and the rates of return on capital may fluctuate over time, historical data, as previously noted, consistently show that capital returns significantly outpace economic growth.

For example, between 1987 and 2013, the global economy grew at an average annual rate of 3.3 percent, while per capita income rose by only 1.4 percent. In stark contrast, the wealth of the richest individuals increased at annual rates between 6.4 percent and 6.8 percent—far outstripping both economic growth and income growth. That disparity is largely driven by the substantial appreciation of assets, such as real estate and stocks, that have outperformed gains in labor income over the same period.

Furthermore, both labor income and capital income are distributed with significant inequality, with capital income inequality far exceeding labor income inequality. For example, the top 10 percent of labor earners typically receive between 25 and 30 percent of total labor income, while the bottom 50 percent also account for roughly 25 to 30 percent of total labor income. In stark contrast, the top 10 percent of capital income earners often capture 50 percent—and sometimes more than 90 percent—of all capital income.

From the data above, we can infer once again that the income disparity between the wealthy and the average individual primarily arises from differences in capital income rather than wage income. In other words, the reason many ordinary individuals feel increasingly left behind is not necessarily due to low wages, but rather to a lack of capital income.

So, how can you increase your capital income? Should everyone strive to become capitalists? There is no one-size-fits-all answer. If you have sufficient startup capital and possess an innovative marketable concept, entrepreneurship can be a viable path for you. However, if you lack either or both, there is no need to be discouraged. You might consider the "lazy person's financial plan" outlined in this book. That strategy requires neither large capital nor innovative business ideas; it simply involves consistently investing your savings into index funds. By doing so, you can effortlessly participate in the capital markets and achieve returns that often surpass average national economic growth. The key ingredient is patience, since the power of compounding takes time to fully unfold, but ultimately will guide you to financial independence.

In the previous discussion, I explored the reasons behind the widening wealth gap between different social groups. But how does that gap expand between regions and even nations? Peruvian economist Hernando De Soto argued that impoverished countries suffer from significant institutional deficiencies that impede their ability to generate and effectively utilize capital. Although individuals in those nations may have savings and assets, they often face obstacles to asserting control over their property, since property rights and transactions in those countries lack strong legal protection.

For example, unclear property rights records for real estate, ambiguous corporate legal statuses, and similar issues create barriers to converting property into universally recognized capital. That obstructs the flow of assets into high-return sectors and limits wealth creation. In countries with these conditions, asset transactions often take place within restricted networks of acquaintances, without access to broader markets. Consequently, these institutional shortcomings become critical constraints on economic growth and wealth generation, further widening the wealth gap between regions and nations.

In *The Mystery of Capital*, De Soto provides a concrete example: In Peru, obtaining a legal ownership certificate for a single parcel of land requires navigating 207 administrative steps across 52 government agencies, a process that takes nearly seven years to complete. That stands in stark contrast to developed Western countries, where every parcel of land, building, and production resource is meticulously recorded in comprehensive ownership registries. Those detailed records are seamlessly integrated into the broader economic framework, which enables the full and efficient utilization of assets in those economies.

Currently, about 80 percent of regions

worldwide face the challenge of insufficient capital, largely because they have yet to develop effective systems to transform their resources into productive capital. Although those areas may have some funds, their lack of necessary business expertise hinders their ability to convert those funds into capital. Furthermore, while those areas may possess substantial assets, most of those remain illiquid—locked in place and unable to flow or be transformed into universally recognized capital.

On a positive note, capital is much scarcer in these regions than in developed Western nations, which often leads to higher rates of return. As a result, capital from developed countries naturally flows into these underdeveloped areas in search of greater profits. Additionally, developing countries may implement targeted policies at strategic moments to attract foreign investment and stimulate economic growth. However, a downside emerges if those policies expire or change, or if foreign investment declines for other reasons. Without the institutional knowledge and capacity to generate capital independently, developing countries risk facing renewed obstacles to sustained economic development.

Since the outbreak of the global COVID pandemic, the saying "A speck of dust in the era is a mountain on an individual's head" has gained widespread resonance. That expression also aptly applies to personal wealth accumulation. If you are fortunate to live in a society with a robust legal system and capital freedom, congratulations! Whether you actively start a business or follow the "lazy person's financial plan" outlined in this book, you have the potential to benefit substantially from capital's dividends.

However, for individuals living in societies constrained by outdated legal frameworks and insufficient capital resources, the path to financial freedom is undeniably more arduous. In light of this, the author's counsel is clear: Either work to change the system or find a way to "escape" it.

The best thing money can buy is financial freedom.

— The Author

Appendix A:
The Rule of 72 Table

Interest Rate (i%)	72 / i	# of years to double (Actual)	% Error
1%	72	69.661	3.36%
2%	36	35.003	2.85%
3%	24	23.45	2.35%
4%	18	17.673	1.85%
5%	14.4	14.207	1.36%
6%	12	11.896	0.87%
7%	**10.286**	**10.245**	**0.40%**
8%	9	9.006	-0.07%
9%	8	8.043	-0.53%
10%	**7.2**	**7.273**	**-1.00%**
11%	6.545	6.642	-1.46%
12%	6	6.116	-1.90%
15%	4.8	4.959	-3.21%
50%	1.44	1.71	-15.79%
100%	0.72	1	-28.00%

Appendix B:

Compound Interest Table

Years	7% Interest Annual Return (K)	7% Interest Annual Balance (K)
1	10.70	10.70
2	11.45	22.15
3	12.25	34.40
4	13.11	47.51
5	14.03	61.53
6	15.01	76.54
7	16.06	92.60
8	17.18	109.78
9	18.38	128.16
10	19.67	**147.84**
...	...	...
20	38.70	**438.65**
...	...	...
30	76.12	**1,010.73**
Total	**1,010.73**	

Compound Interest Formula

Annual Return:

$$10 \times (1 + i)^n$$

Annual Balance:

$$\sum_{1}^{n} \text{Annual Return}$$

Years to Grow = n

Annual Interest Rate = i

Annual Savings = 10 (K)

Appendix C:

28.1 Percent Savings Table

Years	Annual Return (K)	Annual Balance (K)	Target Savings (K)
1	46.88	46.88	925.71
2	48.24	95.12	953.48
3	49.63	144.75	982.09
4	51.06	195.81	1,011.55
5	52.53	248.34	1,041.90
6	54.05	302.39	1,073.15
7	55.61	358.00	1,105.35
8	57.21	415.21	1,138.51
9	58.86	474.07	1,172.66
10	60.56	534.63	1,207.84
...	...	...	...
25	92.78	1,683.70	1,881.78
26	95.45	1,779.16	1,938.24
27	98.21	1,877.36	1,996.38
28	101.04	1,978.40	2,056.27
29	103.95	2,082.36	2,117.96
30	**106.95**	**2,189.31**	**2,181.50**

28.1 Percent Savings Formula

Annual Return:

$$10 \times (28.1/20) \times (1 + i)^{n} \times (1 + j)^{(30 - n)}$$

Annual Balance:

$$\sum_{1}^{n} \text{Annual Return}$$

Target Savings:

$$1000 \times (71.9/80) \times (1 + k)^{n}$$

Years to grow = n

Annual Interest Rate (i) = 7%

Annual Income Increase Rate (j) = 4%

Annual Inflation Rate (k) = 3%

Original Annual Savings = 10 (K)

Original Target Savings = 1000 (K)

Original Savings Percentage = 20%

Original Consumption Percentage = 80%

Adjusted Savings Percentage = 28.1%

Adjusted Consumption Percentage = 71.9%

Appendix D:

40 Percent Savings Table

Years	Annual Return (K)	Annual Balance (K)	Target Savings (K)
1	48.77	48.77	772.50
2	50.17	98.94	795.68
3	51.62	150.56	819.55
4	53.11	203.67	844.13
5	54.64	258.31	869.46
6	56.22	314.52	895.54
7	57.84	372.36	922.41
8	59.51	431.87	950.08
9	61.22	493.09	978.58
10	62.99	556.08	1,007.94
...	...	...	...
17	76.86	1,050.93	1,239.64
18	79.08	1,130.01	1,276.82
19	81.36	1,211.37	1,315.13
20	83.71	1,295.08	1,354.58
21	86.12	1,381.20	1,395.22
22	**88.61**	**1,469.81**	**1,437.08**

40 Percent Savings Formula

Annual Return:

$$10 \times (40/20) \times (1 + i)^{n} \times (1 + j)^{(22 - n)}$$

Annual Balance:

$$\sum_{1}^{n} \text{Annual Return}$$

Target Savings Formula:

$$1000 \times (60/80) \times (1 + k)^{n}$$

Years to grow = n

Annual Interest Rate (i) = 7%

Annual Income Increase Rate (j) = 4%

Annual Inflation Rate (k) = 3%

Original Annual Savings = 10 (K)

Original Target Savings = 1000 (K)

Original Savings Percentage = 20%

Original Consumption Percentage = 80%

Adjusted Savings Percentage = 40%

Adjusted Consumption Percentage = 60%

Appendix E:

50 Percent Savings Table

Years	Annual Return (K)	Annual Balance (K)	Target Savings (K)
1	50.10	50.10	643.75
2	51.55	101.65	663.06
3	53.03	154.68	682.95
4	54.56	209.25	703.44
5	56.14	265.39	724.55
6	57.76	323.14	746.28
7	59.42	382.57	768.67
8	61.14	443.71	791.73
9	62.90	506.61	815.48
10	64.72	571.32	839.95
11	66.58	637.91	865.15
12	68.50	706.41	891.10
13	70.48	776.89	917.83
14	72.51	849.40	945.37
15	74.60	924.01	973.73
16	76.76	1,000.76	1,002.94
17	**78.97**	**1,079.73**	**1,033.03**

50 Percent Savings Formula

Annual Return:

$$10 \times (50/20) \times (1 + i)^{n} \times (1 + j)^{(17 - n)}$$

Annual Balance:

$$\sum_{1}^{n} \text{Annual Return}$$

Target Savings:

$$1000 \times (50/80) \times (1 + k)^{n}$$

Years to grow = n

Annual Interest Rate (i) = 7%

Annual Income Increase Rate (j) = 4%

Annual Inflation Rate (k) = 3%

Original Annual Savings = 10 (K)

Original Target Savings = 1000 (K)

Original Savings Percentage = 20%

Original Consumption Percentage = 80%

Adjusted Savings Percentage = 50%

Adjusted Consumption Percentage = 50%

Appendix F:
70 Percent Savings Table

Years	Annual Return (K)	Annual Balance (K)	Target Savings (K)
1	51.25	51.25	386.25
2	52.73	103.98	397.84
3	54.25	158.24	409.77
4	55.82	214.05	422.07
5	57.43	271.48	434.73
6	59.08	330.57	447.77
7	60.79	391.35	461.20
8	62.54	453.90	475.04
9	**64.35**	**518.24**	**489.29**

70 Percent Savings Formula

Annual Return:

$$10 \times (70/20) \times (1 + i)^{n} \times (1 + j)^{(9 - n)}$$

Annual Balance:

$$\sum_{1}^{n} \text{Annual Return}$$

Target Savings:

$$1000 \times (30/80) \times (1 + k)^{n}$$

Years to grow = n

Annual Interest Rate (i) = 7%

Annual Income Increase Rate (j) = 4%

Annual Inflation Rate (k) = 3%

Original Annual Savings = 10 (K)

Original Target Savings = 1000 (K)

Original Savings Percentage = 20%

Original Consumption Percentage = 80%

Adjusted Savings Percentage = 70%

Adjusted Consumption Percentage = 30%

Contact Author:
weishan.xia@gmail.com

www.ingramcontent.com/pod-product-compliance
Lightning Source LLC
LaVergne TN
LVHW022056200926
848481LV00003B/935